GOLF FITNESS

AN ALL-INCLUSIVE GOLF FITNESS PROGRAM FOR GOLFERS ONLY

Presented by The Team at Golfwell

Published by: Pacific Trust Holdings NZ Ltd., 2017

Thank you to Everkinetic.com for the images.

DISCLAIMER: DO THESE EXERCISES AT YOUR OWN RISK

This Book is a general educational health-related information product and is intended for healthy adults aged 18 and over. This information is not and should not be relied on as professional or physical medical advice, diagnosis, or treatment.

This Book is solely for information and educational purposes and does not constitute medical advice. Please consult a medical or health professional before you begin any exercise, nutrition, fitness, stretching and/or diet program.

There may be risks associated with participating in activities in this book for people who have a health condition or with pre-existing physical or mental health conditions and you should get a professional medical opinion on whether any of the activities is this book are right for you.

Because these risks exist, you should not participate in the activities described in this book if you are in poor health or if you have a pre-existing mental or physical health condition.

Participating in any exercise or exercise program, always involves the possibility of physical injury, heart attack, stroke, or other problems.

If you engage in the Aerobics, All Body Strength and Resistance Training, Core Exercises, Balance Training, Stretching, or any activities or exercises, or anything in this book, you agree that you do so at your own risk, and agree you are voluntarily participating in these activities, assuming all risk of injury to yourself.

Specific results mentioned in this book should be considered extraordinary, and there are no "typical" results. Because individuals differ, results will differ.

We are not a licensed medical care provider and represent we have no expertise in diagnosing, examining, or treating medical conditions of any kind, or in determining the effect of any specific exercise on a medical condition or your physique.

Exercise programs are inherently dangerous and can result in personal injury. Do not start any of these programs if your physician or health care provider advises against it. If you experience faintness, dizziness, pain, or shortness of breath at any time while exercising you should stop immediately.

If you have any concerns or questions about your physical or mental or general health, you should always consult with a physician or other health-care professional. Do not disregard, avoid, or delay obtaining medical or health related advice from your health-care professional because of something you may have read in this book.

Developments in medical research may impact the health, fitness and nutritional advice that appears here. Therefore, no assurance is given that the advice or anything contained in this book will always include the most recent findings or developments with respect to the material.

"Take Care of your body. It's the only place you have to live."

- Jim Rohn

What This Book is About

Why is this Total Golf Fitness Program different?

It's a complete and comprehensive golf fitness program covering the 6 elements of keeping fit: Aerobics, All Body Strength and Resistance Training, Core Exercises, Balance Training, Stretching, and Exercise Variety to Keep You Motivated.

This book also gives you what healthy snacks you should eat playing golf to help you keep focused, as well as information on the diets of top PGA Tour Golfers.

If you want to play better, lose fat, and look great as quickly as possible then you want to read this book.

You're going to learn fitness programs most golfers will never know.

Stronger cardio so you won't get tired playing the last 3 or 4 holes.

Muscle toning with moderate weights and high reps.

A stronger core to make your golf swing easier.

Balance training to keep your shots more consistent.

A ten minute a day stretching program.

Variety in exercising to make it all fun and enjoyable.

Read on, and begin your journey to become a better, leaner, and stronger good-looking golfer!

CONTENTS

INTRODUCTION

Why This Six Element Golf Fitness Program is Different.

This Golf Fitness Program is different since it's a complete and comprehensive golf fitness program covering the basic 6 elements of keeping fit:

1. Aerobics

2. All Body Strength and Resistance Training

3. Core Exercises

4. Balance Training

5. Stretching

6. And, most importantly, *Variety*. We give you ways to keep you motivated and interested in working out.

Most experts agree a well-balanced exercise program should have 6 elements:

1. Aerobics - Cardio Fitness and Training.

Chapter 1 presents a Cardio Fitness program for golfers.

From a golfer's point of view, cardio training is necessary to prevent fatigue during a golf round. Being cardio fit helps your cardio and pulmonary systems become stronger and more able to carry oxygen throughout your body making you less tired, as well as providing many other benefits to your body.

2. Strength and Resistance and Core Exercise Programs

Chapter 2 provides you with Strength and Resistance training exercises, and Core Exercises for golfers. Also included are pre-workout warm up exercises.

Weight training helps increase bone strength and density. It also gives you muscular fitness, and can help you lose fat.

Less fat makes it easier to play 18 holes over a 4 to 5-hour period. (Chapter 10 has information on a proper diet for golfers.)

From a golfer's point of view, having toned muscles allows your brain to have your muscles respond in a coordinated sequence. Chapter 2 also includes a Core Exercise Program for golfers. A good core helps your upper and lower body muscles work together more efficiently.

From a golfer's point of view, your entire body needs to work together in a golf swing and a core exercise program helps your body do that.

3. Additional Strength and Resistance Program and Core Program

Chapter 3 gives you additional golf exercises for Strength Training, and Core Muscle Training so you have a variety of these exercises to work with to keep you motivated.

4. Stability and Balance Training.

Chapter 4 gives you a program to increase your stability and balance.

Statistics show people over 50 years of age are the largest age group engaged in playing golf. As everyone ages, balance and stability exercises are important to maintain and preserve your ability to balance. Being off balance when swinging a golf club is a detriment. Good balancing abilities help you to make and maintain an excellent golf swing.

5. Flexibility Maintenance - Stretching.

Chapter 5 gives you a Stretching Program to increase your flexibility, and ways to maintain your flexibility as you age.

Flexibility decreases as we age. Stretching programs help maintain your flexibility longer, and will also increase your present flexibility.

13

From a golfer's point of view, it's, of course, very important to maintain your flexibility. Making a stretching program an integral part of your exercise program is essential to remaining flexible.

6. Variety in Workouts.

Exercise programs become boring. It's important to know how to keep your exercise program interesting and something you look forward to doing.

Chapter 6 gives you various ways to keep motivated such as having the right music in your ear, doing supersets, changing your routine, etc.

This book also has more information for you.

Included are:

- Warm up exercises when you go to the driving range.
- Driving range practice techniques.
- Warm up exercises prior to playing a golf round.
- Healthy snack suggestions to keep you energized and focused while playing.
- Information on PGA Tour Players diets and how to get trimmer and keep yourself trim.
- And much more....

Fitness and golf are both enjoyable challenges. The exercise programs in this book will help you enjoy being fit and play better golf.

This golf fitness programs are only for golfers. We recommend you use moderate weights with high repetitions.

Golfers tend to live longer.

"There is evidence suggesting golfers live longer than non-golfers, because of improvements in cholesterol levels, and other factors body composition factors, and general wellness, self-esteem and self-worth," according to Dr. Murray, from the University of Edinburgh.

Dr. Murry commented on a Swedish research project which found, "Regular golfers lived an average of five years longer than non-golfers." The Swedish researchers studied the records of The Swedish Golf Federation which has over 600,000 members and compared them to the death records of other Swedes who did not golf. Golfers were about forty per cent less likely to die than others of the same age who didn't play golf.

In the UK, Harry Moorhouse of Norwich, took up golf at the age of 50 and he plays twice a week.

Harry turned 100 in August 2017, and said golf has been his secret for a long and happy life.

"Eat plenty of fruit, drink plenty of water and walk and keep happy. Happy people live longer than miserable people, I think, and I avoid disagreeable people," said Harry.

Reece Rogers of New Zealand who plays regularly at the Awhitu Golf Club took up golf at 85 and reached 100 in March 2017. Reece said,

"It's a challenge against myself. I don't worry about challenging anybody else, but I can challenge myself, so I can finish and say, 'I've done that."

"The Doctor of the Future will give no medicine."

"Instead he will interest his patients in the care of the human frame, in exercise, in fitness, in diet, and in the cause and prevention of disease."

- Thomas Edison.

CHAPTER 1. ELEMENT ONE: AEROBIC TRAINING

"I believe being aerobically fit helps my body recover quickly so that I'm able to compete at the highest level."

- Tiger Woods

Developing aerobic fitness means you will be less tired during a round of golf. Cardio fitness helps you fight off fatigue during a golf round.

You can become aerobically fit by doing cardio on a regular schedule. Activities like swimming, tennis, walking, cycling, jogging, jumping rope, and using cardio machines are all great choices. Dancing and sex are also cardio activities.

The most important aspect is having a program and sticking to it.

Most experts (Mayo Clinic, Cleveland Clinic, and others) agree the time spent on a weekly aerobic program should total at least 75 minutes of intense aerobic activity, or 150 minutes of moderate aerobic activity (per week).

The American Heart Association recommends a minimum of 40 minutes of moderate aerobic exercises 3 or 4 times a week, which totals 120 minutes to 160 minutes per week.

If you don't have a cardio program at present, you need to *gradually* work yourself into a program you can stick with considering your present working and family schedules.

Each cardio program is unique to the individual person according to his age, weight, physical disabilities, etc.

One example of an aerobic program, is the one Greg Norman sticks with. Greg, now in his sixties, works out five times a week.

Greg devotes the first 45 minutes of each session by using different cardio machines. This works out to 225 minutes of aerobic excises per week.

Set your own goals and work out your own program with the help and advice of your medical professional as aerobic training is necessary for your weekly fitness program to give you the energy you need on the golf course, as well as life in general.

The essential point for aerobic/cardio workout is at least 150 minutes a week (i.e., five 30-minute sessions each 7 days).

Aerobic/Cardio sessions do not necessarily mean going to the gym (although cardio machines are very helpful). Types of aerobic/cardio workouts are limitless.

The American Heart Association defines physical exercise as anything that makes your body move and burn calories according to a 2016 report from the AHA.

For example, well known aerobic/cardio exercises are:

Jogging

Climbing stairs

Squats

Jumping Jacks

Burpees

Brisk walking

Most any brisk physical activity.

Look at your lifestyle and develop a regular routine.

CHAPTER 2. ELEMENTS TWO AND THREE: STRENGTH AND RESISTANCE TRAINING, AND CORE EXERCISES

"My goal was always to be the best I could be."

"If you think about it, there is a finality in reaching the top spot. Not only is it hard to get there, but you can't stay forever on that perch."

"But being the best you can be, is infinite."

"There's always room to grow. There's always something new to learn."

"And, there's always something new to do."

- Greg Norman

Golfers, in general, need to avoid bulking up as thick muscles tend to interfere with a smooth flexible golf swing.

Good muscle tone is essential to the golfer. A full body work out session is best to keep your body balanced. You don't want to have one of your muscle groups stronger than another group. In all the exercises, you should only use moderate weights and high repetitions.

Moderate weights and high repetitions (12 to 20 reps per set) lead to toning, flexibility, and strength in your muscle groups.

Heavy weights with low repetitions will bulk up your physique.

The American Heart Association recommends at least two one-hour strength and resistance training sessions per week.

Also, you don't have to do the same gym exercises each session. The important part is making sure you exercise all your muscle groups: Legs, Chest and Shoulders, Back, and Core.

In this Chapter 2, there are weight exercises especially for golfers to evenly balance strength building in all these muscles groups.

Again, you should do 3 exercises for your legs, 3 exercises for your chest and shoulders, 3 exercises for your back, and 3 exercises for your core. Working these 4 muscle groups evenly tends to develop a well-balanced physique.

Visit the gym at least three times a week for a 50-minute session and integrate the gym sessions into your weekly routine.

Again, Chapter 3 has additional Leg, Chest and Shoulder, Back, and Core exercises for you so you can substitute different golf exercises to the original suggested program.

Changing your strength and resistance training program every 4 to 6 weeks will keep you fit and well balanced.

Each exercise is described and a diagram shown along with a suggested number of sets and repetitions.

Pre-routine Strength Training Warm Up

Begin each gym session by warming up before you touch a weight in the gym to avoid injury.

You can get your muscles warm and loose by simply by doing cardio at a moderate pace for 5 to 10 minutes.

You can walk at a fast pace, or jog on a treadmill, pedal on a stationary bicycle, warm up on a rowing machine, or, chose any cardio machine(s) you prefer.

For variety, try using a different cardio machine for warming up before beginning the exercise session.

Golfers need strong and toned legs, and one of the best exercises for legs are squats. Simple squats can be used to warm up prior to your weight workout.

Squats strengthen your leg stabilizer muscles which are important in preventing sports injuries.

Squats also strengthen your ligaments and connective tissues as well as make you more flexible. Squats are great for having flexibility in your ankles and hips which is important to golfers.

Doing squats also creates an anabolic state which promotes muscle building for your entire body by releasing testosterone and human growth hormone.

Doing leg exercises first, especially squats, releases hormones which help all the rest of the muscles of your body work better and grow.

Squats help you keep flexible as you grow older and help you maintain flexibility. Squats are a full body exercise increasing leg strength, and give your core a work out as well.

Although squats mainly work your legs and glutes, they also train the hips and hamstrings. Squats strengthen bones, ligaments, and the tendons throughout the lower body.

Remember, if you feel any pain, stop, and seek medical advice immediately.

Pre-Routine Warm Up Squats with Exercise Band

Stand on an exercise band with your feet shoulder width apart.

Grasp the handles and pull them up level to your shoulders.

Squat down until your thighs (quadriceps) are parallel to the floor.

Slowly raise up to the starting position.

Repeat.

Do 3 sets of 12 repetitions of Exercise Band Squats. Spend any time left of the 5 to 10-minute warm up on another cardio machine (e.g. inclined treadmill brisk walk).

Pre-Routine Warm Up with Speed Squats and Barbell

Here is another Squat Warm Up.

Place an empty barbell on your upper back and stand with your feet slightly wider than your shoulders.

Keep facing forward as you squat downward keeping your weight on your heels.

Descend as far as you can comfortably.

Then raise up quickly.

Repeat to warm up your entire body.

Do 3 sets of 12 repetitions of speed squats. Spend any time left of the 5 to 10-minute warm up on another cardio machine (e.g. stationary bike).

Strength and Resistance Training: Leg Workouts

Barbell Side Squats

Stand up straight holding a barbell on the back of your shoulders. Practice this exercise without weights on the barbell if you're not accustomed to doing side squats.

Place your feet outside your shoulders and angle out your right foot out to the side and prepare to squat using your right leg.

Lower your body using your right leg by bending the knee and hip of your right leg.

Keep your left leg slightly bent as you lower your body.

Return to the starting position. Repeat for 8 repetitions.

Then prepare to squat using your left leg and do the side squat movement with the left leg for 8 repetitions, and so on.

As an alternative, you can do the side step squat movement with dumbbells instead of a barbell.

Do 3 sets of 8 side step lunges with each leg.

Double and Single Leg Glute Bridge

Lie on your back with your knees bent and feet flat on the floor.

Raise your hips off the floor toward the ceiling by pressing your right heels into the floor and raising your hips so that your back and upper body and thighs are in a straight line.

Lower your hips back down to the floor and repeat.

As an alternative, you can do single leg glute bridges by getting into the bridge position and extend your left leg out.

Then raise your hips off the floor toward the ceiling by pressing your right heel into the floor raising your hips with your left leg extended in a straight line with your upper body. Then, lower your hips back down to the floor and repeat.

Switch legs and press your left heel into the floor raising your hips and have your right leg extended in a straight line with your upper body, lower and repeat.

Do 2 sets of 15 repetitions with both legs. Then, do 2 more one legged glute bridge sets with each leg for a total of 6 sets.

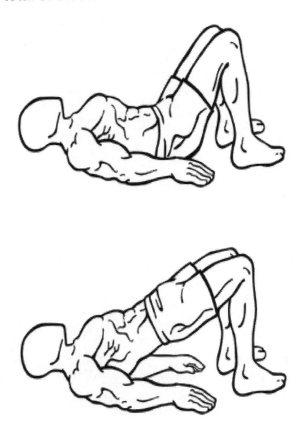

Double and Single Leg Calf Raises on a Leg Press Machine

Adjust the machine to meet your physique and adjust the safety bar to prevent the platform falling in on you since your feet may slip doing calf raises.

Keep your feet shoulder width apart and on the platform.

Your torso and the legs should be at a 90-degree angle. Place your toes and balls of your feet on the platform. You can also have your heels extending off the platform, but be very careful not to slip, as the platform can cause serious injury. Check for a safety pin you can adjust to avoid injury.

Breathe out and press on the platform with the balls of your feet flexing your calves.

Pause at the top, lower, and breathe in as you lower the platform down slowly stretching your calves.

For single leg calf raises, adjust to a lower weight before doing one leg at a time.

Do three sets of 12 repetitions with each leg.

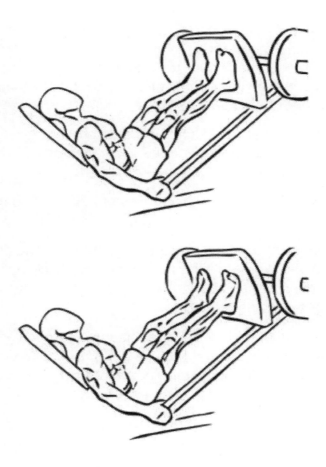

Chest and Shoulder Exercises

Dumbbell Chest Pullover

WARNING: Make sure the plates on the dumbbell are secure so they won't fall off and hit you when you raise it above yourself.

Be aware that if the dumbbell is defective, the plates can fall on you, or use a weight plate you can grasp securely.

Lie on a flat bench with your upper back resting on the bench. Your head should be off the bench.

Have a spotter hand you the dumbbell, or a weight plate after you are lying flat on the bench. Hold the dumbbell or weight plate over your chest with your arms extending straight up.

Lower the dumbbell and breathe in as your lower in an arc formed by your straight arms. Bring the dumbbell up to the starting position. Repeat.

Do 3 sets of 12 repetitions.

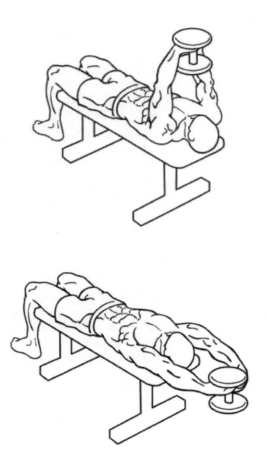

Dumbbell Flys

Sit on a bench holding dumbbells resting on your thighs.

Lie back and raise the dumbbells above you with your palms facing each other.

The dumbbells should be over your nipples as you lower them.

Keep a slight bend in your elbows as you lower your arms out at both sides holding the dumbbells.

Bring the dumbbells down until you feel your chest stretch out.

Pause, then bring them back to the original position above your chest keeping a slight bend in your elbows as your raise them above your chest.

Repeat.

Do 3 sets of 12 repetitions.

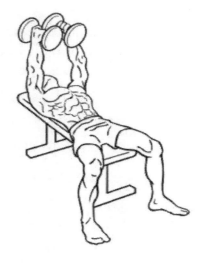

One Arm Military Dumbbell Press with Alternatives

Stand with your right arm holding a dumbbell at shoulder height. Put your left arm on your hip or on something stable. Palms are facing forward.

Press the right-hand dumbbell upward with your right arm until it is fully extended.

Pause and slowly lower it to your chest.

Do the same with your left arm. Repeat.

Alternative: Instead of standing, you can sit on an adjustable bench and do the exercise.

Do the Military Press with a dumbbell in each hand with palms facing forward. Press the dumbbells alternately raising the right dumbbell first, then lowering it to your chest, then raise the left dumbbell, then lower it to your chest, and so on.

Another alternative: Sit on an adjustable bench and extend both of your arms raising the dumbbells at the same time. Touch them together at the top with your palms facing forward. Repeat.

Do 3 sets of 12 repetitions with each arm.

Back Muscle Group Exercises

Standing Upright Rows

This exercise is great for your upper back, shoulders, and biceps.

Grasp a barbell with your palms facing behind you with your hands a few inches inside shoulder width.

Exhale as you raise the barbell to your shoulders in a slow and continuous motion.

Lower the barbell in a slow and continuous motion and exhale as you lower it.

Do 3 sets of 12 repetitions each.

Pull Ups

Use a step or platform to stand on bringing your chin up to the pull up bar.

Grab the pullup bar with your palms facing away from you.

Step off the box or bench, or bend your knees so you can slowly lower yourself down by extending your arms.

Raise yourself up to chin level, pause, and lower yourself down.

As you raise yourself up, pinch your shoulder blades together and tighten your abdominal muscles.

Do as many pull ups as you can. Then set a goal (say one or two more pull ups) for yourself and work up to reach that goal.

Sitting Cable Row

Sit on the Cable machine with your feet flat on the foot platform. Your knees should be bent.

Hold the cable handles with your palms facing each other, or use a V-Bar.

Keep your back straight or slightly leaning forward.

Arch your back and pull the handles toward your chest and breathe out.

Pause when you pull the handles to your chest. Slowly return them extending your arms and breathe out as you do. Repeat.

Caution: Avoid swinging your torso back and forth as you can cause lower back injury.

Do 3 sets of 12 repetitions

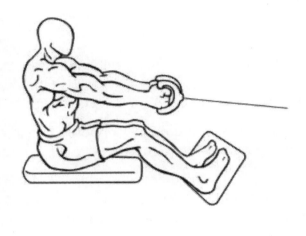

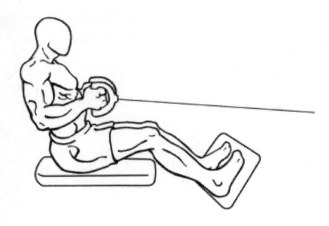

Core Exercises

Side Plank

Lie down sideways on a gym mat supporting your upper body with your forearm perpendicular to your upper body.

Raise your hip off the ground, supporting yourself with your foot and elbow. Straighten out your body in a raised sideways position.

Hold the position for a few seconds, then slowly lower your hips and the sides of your leg to the floor. Repeat.

Work up to raising and lowering yourself to the side plank position for 1 minute on each side (or set a higher or lower goal for yourself).

Work up to raising and lowering yourself to the side plank position for one minute on each side. Or set a higher or lower goal for yourself.

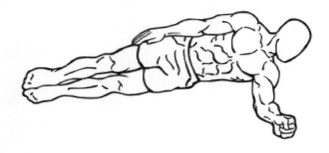

"It is exercise alone that supports the spirits, and keeps the mind in vigor."

> *- Cicero*

Pull Over on a Swiss-Ball

Roll back on a Swiss-Ball with your upper back resting on the ball.

Your feet should be spaced apart flat on the floor giving you stability.

Ask someone to hand you a weighted plate (not old or defective).

Hold the plate up toward the ceiling with your arms extended upward.

In an arcing motion lower the plate with your arms slightly bent behind your head.

Arch your back as you lower it.

Then raise it back to the starting position.

Ask a spotter to take the plate from you when finished.

Do 3 sets of 12 repetitions.

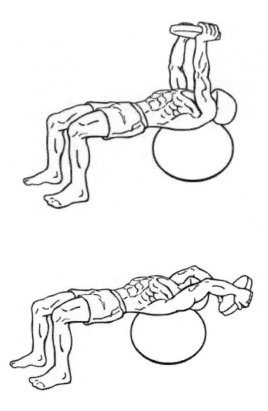

Superman Pilates Exercise (Improves back muscles and your posture)

Begin by lying down on your stomach with your arms extended out in front of you on a mat.

Breathe in and raise your arms and legs slightly off the mat.

Hold the superman position for a few seconds, then lower to the mat and exhale. Repeat.

Work up to raising and lowering yourself for two minutes.

Do 3 sets of 12 repetitions, or work up to do these for two minutes.

CHAPTER 3. ADDITIONAL GOLF EXERCISES

"Strength does not come from winning. Your struggles develop your strengths. When you go through hardships and decide not to surrender, that is strength."

"The resistance you physically fight in working out in the gym, and the resistance you fight in life, builds a strong character."

> *- Arnold Schwarzenegger*

To help keep you motivated, this Chapter has additional exercises you can substitute for the Leg, Chest & Shoulder, Core, and Back Exercises in Chapter 2.

Different exercises are important to change your routine and keep you motivated. Workout become more interesting.

Most of us have a daily routine of getting up in the morning, going to work, coming home, etc. Visualize going to the gym as a vacation from your daily routine. These exercises will help keep you on that vacation.

You should change you exercises if you've been going to the gym on schedule and you don't see any improvement. If you train the same way every time you go to the gym, your body tends to adapt.

Even though it's generally good to change your routine every 4 to 6 weeks, you can change your routine any time any of the exercises become boring. New exercises present new challenges.

You should come out of the gym energized and stimulated. If you find you are not as energized as you were before, substitute new exercises.

More Leg Exercises

Leg Squats

Stand with the barbell supported by your upper back (on your trapezius) muscles.

Face forward and your feet should be turned out and hip distance apart or slightly wider.

Lower yourself by flexing you knees. Your knees will move forward and keep your knees aligned with your feet as you lower yourself.

Keep your torso upright as much as possible and you should continue to look forward as you descend.

Continue down until your thighs are at least parallel to the floor. Push yourself up on the same path using your heels and keep looking forward.

Do 3 sets of 12 repetitions

Leg Extensions

Sit on the machine and adjust the weight and seat to fit your physique. The pad that you will lift with your shins should be comfortably positioned just above your feet. There should be a maximum angle of 90 degrees between you upper and lower legs.

Using your quadriceps, extend your legs out as you exhale.

Pause at the top of the extension.

Slowly lower to the starting position but don't lower more than 90 degrees as it may cause stress on you knee joints.

Repeat.

You can vary this exercise by pointing your toes outward and inward which will work different parts of your quadriceps.

You can also adjust to a lower weight and extend one leg at a time.

Do 3 sets of 12 repetitions.

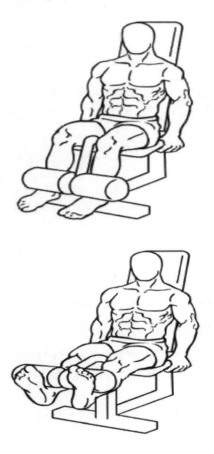

Dumbbell Step Ups with Curl

You should not do this exercise if you have any trouble with your balance.

Unless you are used to doing these, try this exercise without dumbbells until you are comfortable with it.

Then only use light to moderate dumbbells.

Stand holding dumbbells with your palms facing the sides of your legs, and have a low raised platform in front of you.

Step up on the platform using your right leg and raise your left leg up bringing your left knee up.

Curl your arms up by curling the dumbbells toward your shoulders.

Step down and continue stepping up using your left leg (alternate legs with each step) and curling at the top.

Do 3 sets of 8 repetitions alternating legs.

More Chest and Shoulder Exercises

Alternating Dumbbell Bench Press

Sit on a flat bench resting two dumbbells on your thighs.

Roll back on the bench and hold the dumbbells slightly above your chest. Palms should be facing forward.

Press the dumbbell in your right hand upward keeping your wrist straight. Pause at the top then lower your right hand and dumbbell back to the start position.

Press the dumbbell in your left hand upward keeping your wrist straight. Pause at the top then lower your left hand and dumbbell back to the start position. Continue in an alternating manner.

Do 3 sets of 12 repetitions

One Arm Front Cable Raises

Set the pulley to ankle height and select a moderate to low weight. Hold a cable handle in your right hand with your arms down and your palms facing down.

Keep your feet shoulder width apart, and take one step forward. Lean forward slightly for balance.

Extend your right arm upward drawing the handle up to your chest height. Pause at the top, the slowly lower the cable down to the starting position. Repeat. Then do the same with your left arm.

Alternatives: Set both pulleys to ankle height and raise both pulleys with both arms at the same time to chest height then lower it.

Or, raise the pulleys alternately, raising one arm then lowering it, and then raising the other arm, and so on.

Or, grasp the cable handle with one hand with the palm facing forward and upward. With a slight bend in your elbow, twist your upper body pulling the cable handle upward as you would do throwing a ball underhanded for 12 repetitions. Then repeat with the other hand for 12 repetitions, and so on.

Do 3 sets of 12 repetitions with each arm.

Bent Over Low Pulley Rotation

Use a moderate to a low weight.

Bend at the waist keeping your back straight.

Grab the pulley with your left hand and place your right hand on your right thigh above the knee for balance.

With a slight bend in your left elbow, raise the pulley to the side by raising your left arm until it is parallel to the floor. Breathe out as you are pulling up.

Return the cable handle to the starting position and breathe in. Repeat.

Then do the same with the other arm.

Do 3 sets of 12 repetitions with each arm.

Cable Crossovers

Place the cable pulleys in the highest position, select a moderate weight, and grab the cable handles and take one step forward.

Slightly bend your elbows and bend forward. Pull the cable handles down breathing in and bring your hands together at the bottom of the arc.

Then return your arms to the top and breathe out. Keep your arms on the same path as you pull down and return the handles up. starting position. as you breathe out keeping your arms on the same arc.

Repeat.

Variation: Place one hand on the cable handle and put your other hand on your hip or leg for balance. Pull the cable handle down twisting your upper body as you pull the cable handle down in an arc.

Do 3 sets of 12 to 15 repetitions for each side. For one arm cable crossover, do 3 sets of 12 to 15 repetitions with each arm.

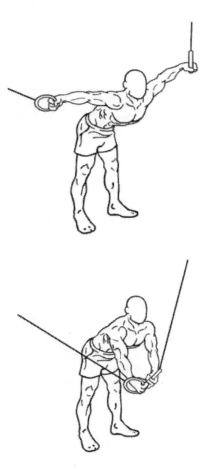

Additional Back Exercises

Bent Over Dumbbell Row

Place a dumbbell on the floor (or hold a dumbbell and hang it down) on the right side of a flat bench.

Put your left knee on the flat bench with your back straight and parallel to the floor.

Pick up the dumbbell with your right hand with your palm facing inward toward you.

Pull the dumbbell up to the side of your chest keeping your back straight and breathe out as you raise the dumbbell.

Slowly lower the dumbbell straight down to the starting position breathing in as you lower the dumbbell.

Repeat.

After completing the set repetitions, switch sides and pull the dumbbell up using your other arm.

Do 3 sets of 12 repetitions with each arm.

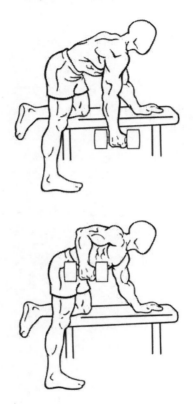

Additional Core Exercises

Abdominal Crunches

Lie down on your back with your calves resting on a bench. Your upper and lower legs should be bent at a 90-degree angle.

Cross your arms on your chest or put them by your sides. Or, put your fingers to your ears and keep your hands on the sides of your head over your ears. Don't force your head up. Raise your torso toward the ceiling. Avoid straining your neck.

Lift your chest toward the ceiling using your abdominal muscles and look up at the ceiling as you raise your upper torso.

Trying to raise your head forward may give you the sensation you're lifting higher, but you really aren't since you only want to raise your torso while keeping your eyes fixed on the ceiling.

Inhale as you raise up.

Lower yourself down slowly and exhale. Repeat.

Do 3 sets of 20 repetitions each.

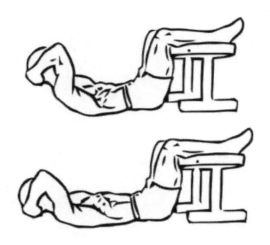

"I don't count my sit ups."

"I only start counting when it hurts."

"Because they're the only ones that count."

> *- Muhammed Ali*

Swiss-Ball Crunches

Swiss-Ball Abdominal Crunches.

Lay back a Swiss-Ball and keeping your balance, adjust yourself so you are balanced with your back supported by the Swiss-Ball.

Cross your arms on your chest, or place your hands on the sides of head over your ears.

Don't pull up with your hands forcing your head up.

Lift your torso up using your abdominal muscles. Trying to raise your head forward may give you the sensation you're lifting higher, but you really aren't. You only want to raise your torso.

Inhale as you raise up.

Lower yourself down slowly and exhale. Repeat.

Do 3 sets of 25 Swiss-Ball crunches

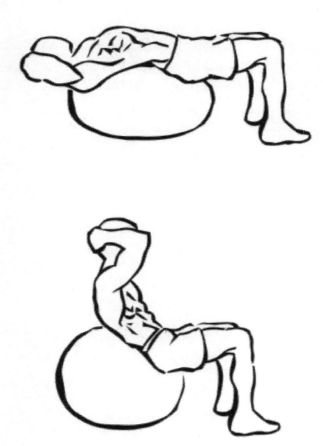

Side Bends with a Dumbbell

Stand up straight with your feet shoulder width apart.

Hold a dumbbell with your right hand. Your palm should be facing inward toward you. Your other hand should be placed on your left hip.

Keep your back straight and look forward. Bend sideways to the right lowering the dumbbell to a comfortable position, then raise it back up the starting position.

Repeat.

Then switch the dumbbell to your left hand and do the side bend on your left side.

Do 3 sets of 15 bends with each arm.

Abdominal Draw In

Get down on your hands and knees on a mat keeping your arms straight.

Align your neck, back and spine parallel with the floor.

Draw your abdominals in while keeping your neck, back and spine straight.

Hold for two seconds, then repeat.

Do 3 sets of 20 repetitions

CHAPTER 4. ELEMENT FOUR: BALANCE TRAINING

Bicep Curl on a Stability Ball

Place a Swiss Ball behind you.

Stand holding two dumbbells at your side. Carefully place the top of your left foot on the top of the Swiss Ball behind you.

Turning your palms to face forward, curl both dumbbells at the same time. Inhale as you curl them.

Slowly lower the dumbbells as you exhale.

Repeat.

Do 3 sets of 12 to 15 repetitions each.

One Leg Squat with Barbell

Place a flat bench behind you. Keep in mind the higher the bench, the greater the difficulty in doing this exercise and keeping your balance. Start with a very low bench, or even a lower stool.

Practice this without the barbell until you are comfortable you can do this exercise.

Place the top of your right foot behind you on a small stool and descend by bending your left knee.

Lower yourself slowly keeping your balance. Then raise up to the starting position. Repeat.

Cease doing this exercise if you cannot control your balance.

Switch legs after completing a set. Then squat with your other leg.

Start with 3 sets of 4 repetitions and work up to 12 repetitions with each leg.

Swiss-Ball Abdominal Pull In

Lie on your stomach as if you are going to do a pushup.

Ask someone to help you place a Swiss-Ball under your knees and shins, or put a Swiss-Ball under your knees and shins if you can manage to do that yourself.

Keeping your back straight, push up with both arms into a raised pushup position.

Pull your knees toward you so the ball goes toward you and under your ankles.

Then extend your legs going back to your original position.

Repeat.

Start with 3 sets of 8 repetitions. Work your way up to 15 receptions or as many as you want to.

Single Leg Balancing Exercises

One Arm Toe Touches

Hold on to a chair or side rail in practicing this exercise until you're proficient.

In a standing position, put your right hand on a rail or other support and raise your right foot slightly off the ground.

Face forward, then extend your right leg out behind you as you bend your torso forward parallel to the ground. Keep your left leg slightly bent as you extend your right leg out behind you.

Reach down with your left hand and touch your left ankle or left toe. Pause, then slowly return to your original standing position.

Repeat touching your left toe and work your way up to raising and lowering touching your left toe 12 times.

Then switch legs and do the same with the other leg by extending your left leg out and bending down to touch your right ankle or right toe with your right hand.

Arabesque

Another single leg balancing exercise is an Arabesque - a well-known common ballet position.

From a standing position, practice going into the arabesque position holding on to a chair, side rail, or other support.

Shift your weight to your right leg and turn your right foot slightly out.

Bend forward extending and gradually raising your left leg keeping your balance. Position yourself so you can extend both of your arms out.

Keep bending forward until your left leg, back and upper torso are parallel to the floor.

Hold the arabesque position for 5 seconds and work your way up to holding it for 30 seconds.

Practice standing on your left leg as well.

CHAPTER 5. ELEMENT FIVE: FLEXIBILITY AND STRETCHING

Stretching is great for everyone, especially for golfers. Daily stretching doesn't take long and makes you more flexible and improves and maintains your golf swing.

Stretching should be done at any time during the day or evening, and it's especially beneficial during or after gym sessions.

You only need to stretch your body to a comfortable point. Don't push the stretch past a comfortable extension. Avoid over twisting or straining, or over bending too far as this can overextend the muscle and cause injury.

There's a tendency to think pushing and straining stretches as far as you can will make you more flexible faster, but the opposite is actually true. It's best only to stretch to where you can feel the limit of the stretch and don't stretch beyond that point. Then hold the stretch for 30 seconds.

It's not how far you extend your stretch. It's doing a regular daily stretching routine that will make you more flexible.

Before beginning this simple stretching routine, warm up by walking or moving around for 5 to 10 minutes.

"Flexibility is crucial to my fitness. Incorporating a good warm-up and cool-down into every session decreases my chances of injury."

"I use both dynamic and static stretching in my training. I've started doing a few yoga sessions which incorporates muscle strength and flexibility."

- Samantha Stosur

Stretch 1:

Sit on a gym mat and place your left ankle over your right knee. Place your right elbow on the side of your left knee.

Extend your left arm behind you and slowly turn to the left. Hold for 30 seconds.

Repeat the stretch on the opposite side.

Stretch 2: Quadricep Stretch.

Turn on your side and grasp your right foot with your right hand and hold for 30 seconds.

Flip over on your right side and repeat the quadricep stretch with the left hand and leg.

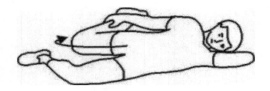

Stretch 3: Oblique and Shoulder Stretch.

Stand and extend your arms over your head then bend your elbows and place your left hand over your right elbow. Bend to your left and hold for 30 seconds.

Repeat this stretch with the other arm.

Additional Simple Stretches:

See the diagram on the opposite page and add any of these stretches.

The first 3 stretches plus these 12 stretches should take under 10 minutes to do each day.

The muscle groups being stretch are shown below the diagram of the stretch.

Gastrocnemius and Soleus = Calf muscles

Psoas = Hip Flexor, a core muscle

Hamstring = Posterior thigh muscle

Adductors = Group of muscles around the hip, core muscles

Quadriceps = Front and side thigh muscles. Hold on to a chair for support when doing this stretch.

Gluteals = Buttocks muscles

Triceps = Large back upper arm muscle

Pectorals = Upper chest muscles

Hold each stretch for 30 seconds.

Gastrocnemius   Soleus   Psoas   Hamstrings

Adductors   Adductors   Adductors   Quadriceps

Gluteals   Triceps   Pectorals

CHAPTER 6. ELEMENT SIX: HOW TO KEEP IT ALL INTERESTING

A University of Florida study found if you keep repeating the same routine, your chances of discontinuing your exercise programs increase. Variety is important in an exercise program.

1. One way to fight boredom is to vary your gym routine every four weeks to six weeks.

The golf exercise program in Chapter 3 of this book has additional exercises you can use to keep you motivated. In Chapter 2, we've given you 3 exercises for each muscle group. That is, there's three exercises for legs, three exercises for chest and shoulders, three exercises for back, and 3 exercises for your core muscles.

2. If counting reps while your work out gets tiring, try counting reps backward. Or, if you're doing a set of say 12 reps, count in 3 groups of 4-counts to total 12 repetitions.

3. Do supersets, which means after you do one set of an exercise, go right into an opposite exercise without pausing.

For example, after doing a set of dumbbell flys for your chest, walk over to the cable machine and without resting, do a set of 12 seated cable rows. Then rest a minute and go back and do another set of dumbbells flys, then an immediate set of cable rows, and so on completing 3 sets of two exercises.

Supersets will keep your heart rate up as well.

4. Listen to different music in your headphones. That is, keep changing your playlist and add new playlists.

A University of Wisconsin (at Lacrosse) study found your "Exercise endurance" increases 15% if you listen to upbeat music while you are working out.

Exercise endurance means you'll be fresher and work out longer with more effort.

5. Having a gym workout partner will help to keep things interesting as well. Your partner may be using lighter or heavier weights, but you can motivate each other and have contests between yourselves. For example, see who can hold a plank or a side plank the longest.

If you and your gym partner are aiming to lose weight, have friendly wagering over who can lose the most weight on a percentage basis, i.e., your very own "Biggest Loser" Contest.

6. Another way to keep things interesting is to set small individual goals for yourself. Seeing your own progress will keep you motivated. Your weight may stay the same, but take photos of yourself every three weeks to see your body shape changing. There's a journal in Appendix One of this book for you to keep track your workouts, weights, etc.

7. If your gym offers aerobic classes or other classes that interest you, try out a class. The first time you join a class may be awkward, but everyone has gone through it.

8. Take your cardio workouts outdoors. Studies have been determined people who exercise outdoors are more energized and less frustrated. Walk, jog, bike, run, or any exercise activity, and see how you feel compared to an indoor gym workout.

9. Join an outdoor boot camp exercise group.

10. Don't get discouraged. Simply know there are good days and bad days to everything you do. Variety will keep you fresh.

11. Try an exercise class. Join a Pilates class which will improve your flexibility and core muscles. Core muscles are extremely important to the golfer.

12. A yoga course will help you stretch and help you maintain flexibility for your golf swing. Tai Chi does this as well.

"I wake up at 4:15 A.M., get some coffee, turn on the news, see what's happening."

"Then I go clickety-clack on the web to see what I missed overnight."

"Then I go to the gym, around 5:15 A.M."

"And I do a very light workout, but who cares."

"I'm socializing with other nice people at the gym."

"Then I go into work, and I'm really awake."

> *- Hoda Kotb, Co-Anchor NBC Today*

CHAPTER 7. DRIVING RANGE WARM UP EXERCISES

Before hitting balls on the range, or before beginning a golf round, warm up your muscles to avoid injury and loosen up.

Following are warm up exercises such as Leg Swings, Arm Swings, Skater Lunges, High Knees, Warm Up Squats, Discuss Throws, etc. Or, do your favorite individual warm up routine - whatever suits you.

Here are just some warm up exercises to get stiffness out of your body and warm up your muscles:

Leg Swings

Do Backward and Forward Leg Swings: Hold on to a stationary object for balance and swing your right leg backwards and forward. Then do the same with your left leg.

Side Leg Swings: Hold on to a stationary object for balance and swing your right leg side to side. Then do the same with your left leg. Do at least 20 Backward and Forward Leg Swings and at least 20 Side to Side Leg Swings.

Arm Swings

Loosen up your arms and shoulders and upper back with arm swings.

Stand with your feet shoulder width apart and swing your arms forward and backward as fast as you can like you were running very fast.

Then swing them side to side twisting your upper torso as you swing your arms.

Or, stand with your feet shoulder width apart and rotate your arms in a circular motion loosening up both your arms and shoulders.

Hold the handle of a golf club with one hand, and club head with the other hand and hold the club out in front of you. Raise one end while you lower the other end, and vice versa back and forth, turning it in front of yourself.

Do at least 20 forward arm swings as if you were running and 20 side to side arms swings, or any arm swings you like to do.

Skater Lunge with Side to Side Arm Swing

Start in a standing position.

Lunge forward with your right leg. As you descend into your lunge, swing your arms as if you are skating.

Then do the same with your left leg.

Alternative method: Lunge forward with your right leg. As you are descending, swing your arms several times from side to side holding the lunge.

Repeat for the left leg swinging your arms back and forth several times. Do at least 20 Skate Lunges.

High Knees

Stand upright with your feet hip distance apart.

Extend your arms out holding a golf club horizontally and parallel to the ground just above your waist.

Your hands should be palms down.

Lift your right knee up to meet your right hand or club shaft and return it to the ground.

Then bring your left knee up to your left hand or club shaft and return it to the ground.

Warm Up Squats

Hold a golf club out in front of you horizontally with the shaft parallel to the ground.

Descend into a squat, and as you are descending raise the golf club above your head.

Descend into each squat as far as you can descend comfortably.

As you raise up from the squat, bring the club back down to the starting position parallel to the ground.

Repeat. Do 3 sets of 10 squats.

Discuss Turns

For right handers: Stand upright with your knees slightly bent and arms at your side.

Imagine you are holding a discuss in your right hand.

Swivel your upper torso and bring your right arm back rotating your shoulders 90 degrees, or as far as you can go comfortably. Lower down as you rotate back bending your knees.

Swing both of your arms as quickly as you can as if you were swiveling to throw and release a discuss. Let your body rotate freely as you throw the imaginary discuss at an upright 45-degree angle. Repeat.

Do 2 sets of 20 discuss turns simulating throwing a discuss.

CHAPTER 8. DRIVING RANGE WARM UP TECHNIQUES BEFORE A ROUND

Many golfers take out driver and hit balls repeatedly to warm up. Generally, there is a tendency to think you want to practice the first shot you're going to hit off the first tee so you can hit your tee shot well.

You temporarily gain a slim confidence which is quickly lost after the round begins. Since repeating shots with a driver repeatedly - making small adjustments each time you hit - will not get all your muscles loose for the round.

You can practice repeating shots or grooving any technique at a different time.

Your objective at the range before a round is to get the muscles you will be using on the course loosened up, as well as develop a smooth and comfortable tempo when swinging.

Concentrate of swinging with a smooth controlled tempo using 70%-80% of your power. Focus on making good contact with the ball.

Don't hit the same shot twice in a row (you don't hit the same shot twice in a row on the course except if you lost a ball or hit out of bounds).

Prior to a round, practice different shots, one at a time, as you would be doing on the course from tee to green.

Pick a target on the range where you want to hit to, and do a pre-shot routine before you hit each shot just as if you were on the course.

Start with your driver if that is the first club you plan to use on the first hole.

Then select another club as if you were playing the course. If the first hole on the course you are about to play is a par 5, hit your fairway wood or utility club next, and before hitting the second shot, select a target or area you want to hit it to.

Then, hit a 9 iron to another selected area. Then assume you're on the next tee and hit driver again.

Practicing different shots each time gets your mind thinking about each shot and your body adjusting to each club, just as you will be doing when playing the round.

Likewise, avoid repetitive chips and putts on the chipping and putting green. Hit only one ball at a time, doing a pre-shot or pre-putt routine before each chip or putt just as you would if you were playing the course.

"Practice, work out, proper nutrition, lots of work on my short game. In golf, that's really where the strokes come off the scorecard."

- Paula Creamer

CHAPTER 9. SNACKS FOR FITNESS, ENERGY AND FOCUSING

It's of course important to be energized and focused during a golf round. Make sure you take healthy snacks with you to avoid becoming tired going into the last 4 holes of a golf round.

Here are suggestions for healthy snacks that give you energy and help you keep focusing. Eating the right foods also keeps you from eating bad foods.

Also, when heart attacks occur on the golf course, statistics show 95% of golf course heart attacks are fatal.

There may not be medical help on the way to you if you begin to have a heart attack on the course, and there may not be defibrillators close by as well.

Here are suggestions for snacks to help you keep energized and focused, and heart healthy:

1. Water. Make sure you're hydrated. Dehydration can occur on hot and humid days and causes muscle cramps, fainting and other bad things. When you become severely dehydrated, your body gets fluid from your blood. This slows down the blood needed for your organs which can become very serious.

2. Bananas. Rich in potassium. Potassium is known to relax the walls of blood vessels and can lower your blood pressure. Potassium also helps your muscles work better.

3. Apples. Florida State University Medical Researchers did a study showing an apple or two a day actually lowered LDL Cholesterol (bad cholesterol).

"We were pleasantly surprised apples so effectively lowered LDL (bad) cholesterol," said study researcher Dr. Bahram H. Arjmandi, PhD, RD, Florida State University.

4. More fruits. Most all fruits will give you energy helping you focus and play a better golf round. Pears, apricots (apricots are rich in iron), oranges, strawberries, peaches, grapes, pineapples slices, etc.

5. Nuts. Natural almonds, macadamia nuts, walnuts, and hazelnuts (all preferably unroasted) have been linked to lower cholesterol. Nuts are

high in protein to give you energy from many vitamins and minerals.

6. Dark Chocolate. Dark Chocolate has caffeine and theobromine which will give you an energy boost. The darker the chocolate, the less sugar it contains.

7. Iron rich snacks. Iron helps you feel more energetic and less fatigued. As explained above, apricots (e.g. dried apricots) are rich in iron and easy to put in your bag to take on the course with you. Other green snacks are peas, broccoli, and raisin.

8. Blueberries are in the superfood category. The USGA has shown blueberries increase your cognitive ability and mental agility. Blueberries are also rich in antioxidants.

"Fitness is not about being better than someone else…. It's about being better than you used to be.

   - Anon.

CHAPTER 10. GOLFER'S DIET

No matter how hard you train, your diet may be an obstacle to your golf fitness.

What and how much you eat depends on your physique. People have different shapes, sizes, etc., and the number of calories required each day varies in accordance with your age, bone structure, height, and metabolism. Delicious food is around everywhere you go, and many people enjoy eating.

Most doctors recommend consulting with your personal physician to set realistic goals if you're seeking weight loss as well as a good diet. Setting small goals and reaching those goals gives you a positive feeling of success which motivates you to follow the diet.

If you study the diets of what well known winning golfers eat, you gain insight into healthy eating habits for golfers.

For example, Jordan Spieth has revealed he eats a vegetable omelet with baked sweet potato for breakfast.

For lunch, he'll eat lean fish, more vegetables, brown rice, and lentils. And for dinner, he'll eat a protein like red meat with more vegetables, quinoa, and for snacks on the course, he like granola.

Tiger Woods followed a similar simple diet with an egg omelet and vegetables for breakfast, and ate lean meats, seafood, fruits and vegetables and he avoided junk food.

Rory McIlroy who has a body fat index under 10% said,

"Everything in moderation is my motto."

"I don't cut out anything. If I feel I want some chocolate, I'll have some chocolate. If I want a burger, I'll have a burger, but I wouldn't have a burger every day."

"I'm not very strict with my diet. Probably should be a little stricter if I'm honest, but you're allowed a treat occasionally, so try to keep it like that."

Bernhard Langer revealed a lot about his diet and keeping fit. He said,

"I think one of the keys is to keep the metabolism going."

"You need to eat constantly, not large portions but you need to eat constantly, and a lot of people don't seem to agree with that."

Langer eats bananas, nuts, and other fruits on the course.

Langer says, "I must snack. If I don't, my blood sugar level gets low and I get a little fatigued."

"I don't focus as well, so I need to have stuff with me something to keep you going."

Langer loves to work out as well and enjoys stretching.

"I've worked out all my life. I enjoy working out. I do a lot more when I'm home than when I'm out on tour."

"I stretch twice a day, mornings and evenings, and try and get a workout here and there, even when I'm on tour, some cardio, some weights."

Langer avoids heavy weights. "I've never done really heavy weights."

Langer had back problems too with two bulging discs, and found stretching and working out helped him overcome those. "I stretch and work out in order to stay in shape."

If you want to get yourself trim and stronger, the bottom line on diets is summarized by Michael Matthews in his bestselling book, "Bigger, Leaner Stronger."

"When you give your body more calories than it burns off, it stores fat."

Matthew goes on to add, "When you give your body less calories than it burns throughout the day, it must make up for that deficit by burning its own energy stores (fat), which leads to fat loss."

Being overweight makes you less flexible and golf fit. If you are overweight. You are simply eating too much of the wrong foods and don't spend the daily energy to using up the extra calories.

So, if you want to trim down, you must have your body expend more calories than you take in. Matthews recommends sticking to lean meats and avoiding saturated fats.

Avoid processed foods so it is easier for your body to lose weight. Processed foods are breads, pancakes, bagels, crackers, pretzels, etc.

Other foods to avoid (or seldom eat) making it easier for your body to lose weight are soft drinks with a lot of sugar, fruit juices, pies, cakes, cookies, sugar sweetened candies, ice cream, etc.

It's best to avoid fatty foods such as butter, cheese, mayonnaise, etc. Healthy fats are good for you such as olive oil, avocados, walnuts, salmon, etc.

Generally, each person has their own lifestyle. Some lead active lifestyles and expend a lot of energy, while others lead sedentary lifestyles spending less energy. You have to adjust your food intake accordingly.

The essential point is to eat less calories than your body expends daily and to eat natural foods and avoid processed foods. That will keep you trim and give your body a good look.

"I exercise because somehow completely exhausting myself is the most relaxing part of my day."

> *- Anon.*

In conclusion, if you follow the programs in this book, you will be spending more energy and using more calories in your daily life and on your way to a new you.

You will look better, feel better and play golf better.

About the Authors: We are in New Zealand and have played, studied, researched, and enjoyed golf all our lives. There is a demand and need for a comprehensive golf fitness program (for golfers only) to maintain enjoyment of the game as we age.

This book is a complete source of information for golf fitness with comprehensive exercise programs for increased flexibility and flexibility maintenance, Aerobic/Cardio fitness, Strength and Resistance Training, Core exercises, Balance exercises, Motivational concepts, Diet information, and much more.

We hope you enjoyed the book.

Thank you for reading this book.

If you follow the programs, you will be on your way to feeling and playing better, as well as looking better.

Team Golfwell also thanks Everkinetic.com for the exercise images.

If you enjoyed reading this book, please leave us a review on Amazon. We read all our reviews and we hope this book helps you and want your comments.

Keep track of your progress in the Journal for Tracking Your Workouts that follows. Review your progress every six weeks.

Best to you.

Team Golfwell

Appendix: Journal for Tracking Your Golf Work Outs

Abbreviations for Golf Exercises:

LEGS (Do them in this order)

Barbell Side Squats = BBS p. 29

Double and Single Leg Glute Bridge = GB p. 31

Calf Raises = CR p. 33

CHEST AND SHOULDERS:

Dumbbell Pullover = DP p. 35

Dumbbell Flys = DF p. 37

One Arm Military Dumbbell Press = MDP p. 39

BACK:

Standing Upright Rows = SUR p. 41

Pull Ups = PU p. 43

Sitting Cable Row = SCR p. 45

CORE:

Side Plank = SP p. 47

Date: _____

Body Weight: _____

Exercise   Weight   Sets   # of Reps

BBS_____

GB_____

CR_____

DP_____

DF_____

MDP_____

SUR_____

PU_____

SCR_____

SP_____

PO_____

SM_____

_____

_____

_____

_____

_____

_____

"Golf Fitness" by Team Golfwell

Date: _____

Body Weight: _____

<u>Exercise</u>   <u>Weight</u>   <u>Sets</u>   <u># of Reps</u>

BBS_____

GB_____

CR_____

DP_____

DF_____

MDP_____

SUR_____

PU_____

SCR_____

SP_____

PO_____

SM_____

_____

_____

_____

_____

_____

_____

Date: _____

Body Weight: _____

Exercise	Weight	Sets	# of Reps
BBS_____
GB_____
CR_____
DP_____
DF_____
MDP_____
SUR_____
PU_____
SCR_____
SP_____
PO_____
SM_____

_____

_____

_____

_____

_____

_____

Date: _____

Body Weight: _____

Exercise   Weight   Sets   # of Reps

BBS_____

GB_____

CR_____

DP_____

DF_____

MDP_____

SUR_____

PU_____

SCR_____

SP_____

PO_____

SM_____

_____

_____

_____

_____

_____

_____

Date: _____

Body Weight: _____

Exercise	Weight	Sets	# of Reps
BBS			
GB			
CR			
DP			
DF			
MDP			
SUR			
PU			
SCR			
SP			
PO			
SM			

Date: _____

Body Weight: _____

Exercise	Weight	Sets	# of Reps
BBS_____
GB_____
CR_____
DP_____
DF_____
MDP_____
SUR_____
PU_____
SCR_____
SP_____
PO_____
SM_____

_____

_____

_____

_____

_____

_____

"Golf Fitness" by Team Golfwell

Date: _____

Body Weight: _____

<u>Exercise</u>   Weight   Sets   # of Reps

BBS_____

GB_____

CR_____

DP_____

DF_____

MDP_____

SUR_____

PU_____

SCR_____

SP_____

PO_____

SM_____

_____

_____

_____

_____

_____

_____

Date: _____

Body Weight: _____

Exercise   Weight   Sets   # of Reps

BBS_____

GB_____

CR_____

DP_____

DF_____

MDP_____

SUR_____

PU_____

SCR_____

SP_____

PO_____

SM_____

_____

_____

_____

_____

_____

_____

Date: _____

Body Weight: _____

<u>Exercise</u>   <u>Weight</u>   <u>Sets</u>   <u># of Reps</u>

BBS_____

GB_____

CR_____

DP_____

DF_____

MDP_____

SUR_____

PU_____

SCR_____

SP_____

PO_____

SM_____

_____

_____

_____

_____

_____

_____

Date: _____

Body Weight: _____

Exercise	Weight	Sets	# of Reps
BBS_____
GB_____
CR_____
DP_____
DF_____
MDP_____
SUR_____
PU_____
SCR_____
SP_____
PO_____
SM_____

_____

_____

_____

_____

_____

_____

Date: _____

Body Weight: _____

Exercise   Weight   Sets   # of Reps

BBS_____

GB_____

CR_____

DP_____

DF_____

MDP_____

SUR_____

PU_____

SCR_____

SP_____

PO_____

SM_____

_____

_____

_____

_____

_____

_____

Date: _____

Body Weight: _____

<u>Exercise</u>   <u>Weight</u>   <u>Sets</u>   <u># of Reps</u>

BBS_____

GB_____

CR_____

DP_____

DF_____

MDP_____

SUR_____

PU_____

SCR_____

SP_____

PO_____

SM_____

_____

_____

_____

_____

_____

_____

Date: _____

Body Weight: _____

<u>Exercise</u>   <u>Weight</u>   <u>Sets</u>   <u># of Reps</u>
BBS_____

GB_____

CR_____

DP_____

DF_____

MDP_____

SUR_____

PU_____

SCR_____

SP_____

PO_____

SM_____

_____

_____

_____

_____

_____

_____

Date: _____

Body Weight: _____

Exercise   Weight   Sets   # of Reps

BBS_____

GB_____

CR_____

DP_____

DF_____

MDP_____

SUR_____

PU_____

SCR_____

SP_____

PO_____

SM_____

_____

_____

_____

_____

_____

_____

Date: _____

Body Weight: _____

Exercise   Weight   Sets   # of Reps

BBS_____

GB_____

CR_____

DP_____

DF_____

MDP_____

SUR_____

PU_____

SCR_____

SP_____

PO_____

SM_____

_____

_____

_____

_____

_____

_____

Date: _____

Body Weight: _____

Exercise	Weight	Sets	# of Reps
BBS_____	_____	_____	_____
GB_____	_____	_____	_____
CR_____	_____	_____	_____
DP_____	_____	_____	_____
DF_____	_____	_____	_____
MDP_____	_____	_____	_____
SUR_____	_____	_____	_____
PU_____	_____	_____	_____
SCR_____	_____	_____	_____
SP_____	_____	_____	_____
PO_____	_____	_____	_____
SM_____	_____	_____	_____

_____

_____

_____

_____

_____

_____

Date: _____

Body Weight: _____

<u>Exercise</u>   <u>Weight</u>   <u>Sets</u>   <u># of Reps</u>

BBS_____

GB_____

CR_____

DP_____

DF_____

MDP_____

SUR_____

PU_____

SCR_____

SP_____

PO_____

SM_____

_____

_____

_____

_____

_____

_____

Date: _____

Body Weight: _____

<u>Exercise</u>   <u>Weight</u>   <u>Sets</u>   <u># of Reps</u>

BBS_____

GB_____

CR_____

DP_____

DF_____

MDP_____

SUR_____

PU_____

SCR_____

SP_____

PO_____

SM_____

_____

_____

_____

_____

_____

_____

Date: _____

Body Weight: _____

Exercise   Weight   Sets   # of Reps

BBS_____

GB_____

CR_____

DP_____

DF_____

MDP_____

SUR_____

PU_____

SCR_____

SP_____

PO_____

SM_____

_____

_____

_____

_____

_____

_____

Date: _____

Body Weight: _____

Exercise_____ Weight____Sets____# of Reps
BBS_____

GB_____

CR_____

DP_____

DF_____

MDP_____

SUR_____

PU_____

SCR_____

SP_____

PO_____

SM_____

_____

_____

_____

_____

_____

_____

Date: _____

Body Weight: _____

<u>Exercise</u>   <u>Weight</u>   <u>Sets</u>   <u># of Reps</u>

BBS_____

GB_____

CR_____

DP_____

DF_____

MDP_____

SUR_____

PU_____

SCR_____

SP_____

PO_____

SM_____

_____

_____

_____

_____

_____

_____

Date: _____

Body Weight: _____

Exercise	Weight	Sets	# of Reps

BBS_____

GB_____

CR_____

DP_____

DF_____

MDP_____

SUR_____

PU_____

SCR_____

SP_____

PO_____

SM_____

_____

_____

_____

_____

_____

_____

Date: _____

Body Weight: _____

Exercise	Weight	Sets	# of Reps
BBS			
GB			
CR			
DP			
DF			
MDP			
SUR			
PU			
SCR			
SP			
PO			
SM			

Date: _____

Body Weight: _____

Exercise	Weight	Sets	# of Reps
BBS_____
GB_____
CR_____
DP_____
DF_____
MDP_____
SUR_____
PU_____
SCR_____
SP_____
PO_____
SM_____

_____

_____

_____

_____

_____

_____

Date: _____

Body Weight: _____

Exercise   Weight   Sets   # of Reps

BBS_____

GB_____

CR_____

DP_____

DF_____

MDP_____

SUR_____

PU_____

SCR_____

SP_____

PO_____

SM_____

_____

_____

_____

_____

_____

_____

Date: _____

Body Weight: _____

Exercise	Weight	Sets	# of Reps

BBS_____

GB_____

CR_____

DP_____

DF_____

MDP_____

SUR_____

PU_____

SCR_____

SP_____

PO_____

SM_____

_____

_____

_____

_____

_____

_____

_____

Date: _____

Body Weight: _____

Exercise	Weight	Sets	# of Reps
BBS			
GB			
CR			
DP			
DF			
MDP			
SUR			
PU			
SCR			
SP			
PO			
SM			

Date: _____

Body Weight: _____

Exercise   Weight   Sets   # of Reps
BBS_____

GB_____

CR_____

DP_____

DF_____

MDP_____

SUR_____

PU_____

SCR_____

SP_____

PO_____

SM_____

_____

_____

_____

_____

_____

_____

Date: _____

Body Weight: _____

Exercise   Weight   Sets   # of Reps

BBS_____

GB_____

CR_____

DP_____

DF_____

MDP_____

SUR_____

PU_____

SCR_____

SP_____

PO_____

SM_____

_____

_____

_____

_____

_____

_____

Date: _____

Body Weight: _____

Exercise _____ Weight ___ Sets ___ # of Reps

BBS_____

GB_____

CR_____

DP_____

DF_____

MDP_____

SUR_____

PU_____

SCR_____

SP_____

PO_____

SM_____

_____

_____

_____

_____

_____

_____

Date: _____

Body Weight: _____

Exercise	Weight	Sets	# of Reps
BBS_____
GB_____
CR_____
DP_____
DF_____
MDP_____
SUR_____
PU_____
SCR_____
SP_____
PO_____
SM_____

_____

_____

_____

_____

_____

_____

Date: _____

Body Weight: _____

Exercise	Weight	Sets	# of Reps

BBS_____

GB_____

CR_____

DP_____

DF_____

MDP_____

SUR_____

PU_____

SCR_____

SP_____

PO_____

SM_____

_____

_____

_____

_____

_____

_____

Date: _____

Body Weight: _____

Exercise	Weight	Sets	# of Reps
BBS
GB
CR
DP
DF
MDP
SUR
PU
SCR
SP
PO
SM

Date: _____

Body Weight: _____

<u>Exercise</u>   <u>Weight</u> <u>Sets</u> <u># of Reps</u>

BBS_____

GB_____

CR_____

DP_____

DF_____

MDP_____

SUR_____

PU_____

SCR_____

SP_____

PO_____

SM_____

_____

_____

_____

_____

_____

_____

Date: _____

Body Weight: _____

<u>Exercise</u>   <u>Weight</u>   <u>Sets</u>   <u># of Reps</u>

BBS_____

GB_____

CR_____

DP_____

DF_____

MDP_____

SUR_____

PU_____

SCR_____

SP_____

PO_____

SM_____

_____

_____

_____

_____

_____

_____

Date: _____

Body Weight: _____

Exercise	Weight	Sets	# of Reps
BBS_____			
GB_____			
CR_____			
DP_____			
DF_____			
MDP_____			
SUR_____			
PU_____			
SCR_____			
SP_____			
PO_____			
SM_____			

_____

_____

_____

_____

_____

_____

Date: _____

Body Weight: _____

Exercise   Weight   Sets   # of Reps

BBS_____

GB_____

CR_____

DP_____

DF_____

MDP_____

SUR_____

PU_____

SCR_____

SP_____

PO_____

SM_____

_____

_____

_____

_____

_____

_____

Date: _____

Body Weight: _____

<u>Exercise</u>   <u>Weight</u>   <u>Sets</u>   <u># of Reps</u>

BBS_____

GB_____

CR_____

DP_____

DF_____

MDP_____

SUR_____

PU_____

SCR_____

SP_____

PO_____

SM_____

_____

_____

_____

_____

_____

_____

Date: _____

Body Weight: _____

Exercise	Weight	Sets	# of Reps
BBS_____
GB_____
CR_____
DP_____
DF_____
MDP_____
SUR_____
PU_____
SCR_____
SP_____
PO_____
SM_____

_____

_____

_____

_____

_____

_____

Date: _____

Body Weight: _____

Exercise   Weight   Sets # of Reps

BBS_____

GB_____

CR_____

DP_____

DF_____

MDP_____

SUR_____

PU_____

SCR_____

SP_____

PO_____

SM_____

_____

_____

_____

_____

_____

_____

Date: _____

Body Weight: _____

Exercise	Weight	Sets	# of Reps
BBS_____
GB_____
CR_____
DP_____
DF_____
MDP_____
SUR_____
PU_____
SCR_____
SP_____
PO_____
SM_____

_____

_____

_____

_____

_____

_____

Date: _____

Body Weight: _____

Exercise   Weight   Sets   # of Reps

BBS_____

GB_____

CR_____

DP_____

DF_____

MDP_____

SUR_____

PU_____

SCR_____

SP_____

PO_____

SM_____

_____

_____

_____

_____

_____

_____

Date: _____

Body Weight: _____

Exercise	Weight	Sets	# of Reps
BBS			
GB			
CR			
DP			
DF			
MDP			
SUR			
PU			
SCR			
SP			
PO			
SM			

_____

_____

_____

_____

_____

_____

Date: _____

Body Weight: _____

Exercise   Weight   Sets   # of Reps
BBS_____

GB_____

CR_____

DP_____

DF_____

MDP_____

SUR_____

PU_____

SCR_____

SP_____

PO_____

SM_____

_____

_____

_____

_____

_____

_____

Date: _____

Body Weight: _____

Exercise   Weight   Sets   # of Reps

BBS_____

GB_____

CR_____

DP_____

DF_____

MDP_____

SUR_____

PU_____

SCR_____

SP_____

PO_____

SM_____

_____

_____

_____

_____

_____

_____

Date: _____

Body Weight: _____

Exercise Weight Sets # of Reps

BBS_____

GB_____

CR_____

DP_____

DF_____

MDP_____

SUR_____

PU_____

SCR_____

SP_____

PO_____

SM_____

_____

_____

_____

_____

_____

_____

Date: _____

Body Weight: _____

Exercise   Weight   Sets   # of Reps

BBS_____

GB_____

CR_____

DP_____

DF_____

MDP_____

SUR_____

PU_____

SCR_____

SP_____

PO_____

SM_____

_____

_____

_____

_____

_____

_____

Date: _____

Body Weight: _____

Exercise   Weight   Sets # of Reps

BBS_____

GB_____

CR_____

DP_____

DF_____

MDP_____

SUR_____

PU_____

SCR_____

SP_____

PO_____

SM_____

_____

_____

_____

_____

_____

_____

Date: _____

Body Weight: _____

Exercise	Weight	Sets	# of Reps

BBS_____

GB_____

CR_____

DP_____

DF_____

MDP_____

SUR_____

PU_____

SCR_____

SP_____

PO_____

SM_____

_____

_____

_____

_____

_____

_____

Date: _____

Body Weight: _____

Exercise   Weight   Sets   # of Reps

BBS_____

GB_____

CR_____

DP_____

DF_____

MDP_____

SUR_____

PU_____

SCR_____

SP_____

PO_____

SM_____

_____

_____

_____

_____

_____

_____

Date: _____

Body Weight: _____

Exercise   Weight   Sets   # of Reps
BBS_____

GB_____

CR_____

DP_____

DF_____

MDP_____

SUR_____

PU_____

SCR_____

SP_____

PO_____

SM_____

_____

_____

_____

_____

_____

_____

Date: _____

Body Weight: _____

<u>Exercise</u>   <u>Weight</u> <u>Sets</u> <u># of Reps</u>

BBS_____

GB_____

CR_____

DP_____

DF_____

MDP_____

SUR_____

PU_____

SCR_____

SP_____

PO_____

SM_____

_____

_____

_____

_____

_____

_____

Date: _____

Body Weight: _____

<u>Exercise</u>   <u>Weight</u>   <u>Sets</u>   <u># of Reps</u>
BBS_____

GB_____

CR_____

DP_____

DF_____

MDP_____

SUR_____

PU_____

SCR_____

SP_____

PO_____

SM_____

_____

_____

_____

_____

_____

_____

Date: _____

Body Weight: _____

Exercise   Weight   Sets   # of Reps

BBS_____

GB_____

CR_____

DP_____

DF_____

MDP_____

SUR_____

PU_____

SCR_____

SP_____

PO_____

SM_____

_____

_____

_____

_____

_____

_____

Date: _____

Body Weight: _____

Exercise	Weight	Sets	# of Reps
BBS			
GB			
CR			
DP			
DF			
MDP			
SUR			
PU			
SCR			
SP			
PO			
SM			

"Golf Fitness" by Team Golfwell

Date: _____

Body Weight: _____

Exercise   Weight   Sets   # of Reps

BBS_____

GB_____

CR_____

DP_____

DF_____

MDP_____

SUR_____

PU_____

SCR_____

SP_____

PO_____

SM_____

_____

_____

_____

_____

_____

_____

Date: _____

Body Weight: _____

<u>Exercise</u>   <u>Weight</u>   <u>Sets</u>   <u># of Reps</u>
BBS_____

GB_____

CR_____

DP_____

DF_____

MDP_____

SUR_____

PU_____

SCR_____

SP_____

PO_____

SM_____

_____

_____

_____

_____

_____

_____

Date: _____

Body Weight: _____

Exercise   Weight   Sets   # of Reps

BBS_____

GB_____

CR_____

DP_____

DF_____

MDP_____

SUR_____

PU_____

SCR_____

SP_____

PO_____

SM_____

_____

_____

_____

_____

_____

_____

Date: _____

Body Weight: _____

<u>Exercise</u>   <u>Weight</u>   <u>Sets</u>   <u># of Reps</u>

BBS_____

GB_____

CR_____

DP_____

DF_____

MDP_____

SUR_____

PU_____

SCR_____

SP_____

PO_____

SM_____

_____

_____

_____

_____

_____

_____

Date: _____

Body Weight: _____

Exercise   Weight   Sets   # of Reps

BBS_____

GB_____

CR_____

DP_____

DF_____

MDP_____

SUR_____

PU_____

SCR_____

SP_____

PO_____

SM_____

_____

_____

_____

_____

_____

_____

Date: _____

Body Weight: _____

<u>Exercise</u>   <u>Weight</u>   <u>Sets</u>   <u># of Reps</u>
BBS_____

GB_____

CR_____

DP_____

DF_____

MDP_____

SUR_____

PU_____

SCR_____

SP_____

PO_____

SM_____

_____

_____

_____

_____

_____

_____

Date: _____

Body Weight: _____

<u>Exercise</u>   <u>Weight</u>   <u>Sets</u>   <u># of Reps</u>
BBS_____

GB_____

CR_____

DP_____

DF_____

MDP_____

SUR_____

PU_____

SCR_____

SP_____

PO_____

SM_____

_____

_____

_____

_____

_____

_____

Date: _____

Body Weight: _____

<u>Exercise</u>   <u>Weight</u>   <u>Sets</u>   <u># of Reps</u>

BBS_____

GB_____

CR_____

DP_____

DF_____

MDP_____

SUR_____

PU_____

SCR_____

SP_____

PO_____

SM_____

_____

_____

_____

_____

_____

_____

Date: _____

Body Weight: _____

Exercise	Weight	Sets	# of Reps
BBS_____			
GB_____			
CR_____			
DP_____			
DF_____			
MDP_____			
SUR_____			
PU_____			
SCR_____			
SP_____			
PO_____			
SM_____			

_____

_____

_____

_____

_____

_____

Date: _____

Body Weight: _____

Exercise   Weight   Sets   # of Reps
BBS_____

GB_____

CR_____

DP_____

DF_____

MDP_____

SUR_____

PU_____

SCR_____

SP_____

PO_____

SM_____

_____

_____

_____

_____

_____

_____

Date: _____

Body Weight: _____

<u>Exercise</u>   <u>Weight</u>   <u>Sets</u>   <u># of Reps</u>
BBS_____

GB_____

CR_____

DP_____

DF_____

MDP_____

SUR_____

PU_____

SCR_____

SP_____

PO_____

SM_____

_____

_____

_____

_____

_____

_____

Date: _____

Body Weight: _____

Exercise	Weight	Sets	# of Reps
BBS			
GB			
CR			
DP			
DF			
MDP			
SUR			
PU			
SCR			
SP			
PO			
SM			

Date: _____

Body Weight: _____

Exercise	Weight	Sets	# of Reps
BBS_____			
GB_____			
CR_____			
DP_____			
DF_____			
MDP_____			
SUR_____			
PU_____			
SCR_____			
SP_____			
PO_____			
SM_____			

_____

_____

_____

_____

_____

_____

Date: _____

Body Weight: _____

Exercise	Weight	Sets	# of Reps
BBS_____
GB_____
CR_____
DP_____
DF_____
MDP_____
SUR_____
PU_____
SCR_____
SP_____
PO_____
SM_____

_____

_____

_____

_____

_____

_____

Date: _____

Body Weight: _____

Exercise   Weight   Sets   # of Reps

BBS_____

GB_____

CR_____

DP_____

DF_____

MDP_____

SUR_____

PU_____

SCR_____

SP_____

PO_____

SM_____

_____

_____

_____

_____

_____

_____

Date: _____

Body Weight: _____

<u>Exercise</u>   <u>Weight</u>   <u>Sets</u>   <u># of Reps</u>
BBS_____

GB_____

CR_____

DP_____

DF_____

MDP_____

SUR_____

PU_____

SCR_____

SP_____

PO_____

SM_____

_____

_____

_____

_____

_____

_____

Date: _____

Body Weight: _____

Exercise	Weight	Sets	# of Reps
BBS _____			
GB _____			
CR _____			
DP _____			
DF _____			
MDP _____			
SUR _____			
PU _____			
SCR _____			
SP _____			
PO _____			
SM _____			

_____

_____

_____

_____

_____

_____

Date: _____

Body Weight: _____

<u>Exercise</u>   <u>Weight</u>   <u>Sets</u>   <u># of Reps</u>

BBS_____

GB_____

CR_____

DP_____

DF_____

MDP_____

SUR_____

PU_____

SCR_____

SP_____

PO_____

SM_____

_____

_____

_____

_____

_____

_____

Date: _____

Body Weight: _____

Exercise	Weight	Sets	# of Reps
BBS			
GB			
CR			
DP			
DF			
MDP			
SUR			
PU			
SCR			
SP			
PO			
SM			

Date: _____

Body Weight: _____

Exercise   Weight   Sets   # of Reps

BBS_____

GB_____

CR_____

DP_____

DF_____

MDP_____

SUR_____

PU_____

SCR_____

SP_____

PO_____

SM_____

_____

_____

_____

_____

_____

_____

Date: _____

Body Weight: _____

Exercise	Weight	Sets	# of Reps

BBS_____

GB_____

CR_____

DP_____

DF_____

MDP_____

SUR_____

PU_____

SCR_____

SP_____

PO_____

SM_____

_____

_____

_____

_____

_____

_____

Date: _____

Body Weight: _____

<u>Exercise</u>   <u>Weight</u>   <u>Sets</u>   <u># of Reps</u>

BBS_____

GB_____

CR_____

DP_____

DF_____

MDP_____

SUR_____

PU_____

SCR_____

SP_____

PO_____

SM_____

_____

_____

_____

_____

_____

_____

Date: _____

Body Weight: _____

<u>Exercise</u>   <u>Weight</u>   <u>Sets</u>   <u># of Reps</u>
BBS_____

GB_____

CR_____

DP_____

DF_____

MDP_____

SUR_____

PU_____

SCR_____

SP_____

PO_____

SM_____

_____

_____

_____

_____

_____

_____

Date: _____

Body Weight: _____

<u>Exercise</u>   <u>Weight</u>   <u>Sets</u>   <u># of Reps</u>

BBS_____

GB_____

CR_____

DP_____

DF_____

MDP_____

SUR_____

PU_____

SCR_____

SP_____

PO_____

SM_____

_____

_____

_____

_____

_____

_____

Date: _____

Body Weight: _____

<u>Exercise</u>   <u>Weight</u>   <u>Sets</u>   <u># of Reps</u>

BBS_____

GB_____

CR_____

DP_____

DF_____

MDP_____

SUR_____

PU_____

SCR_____

SP_____

PO_____

SM_____

_____

_____

_____

_____

_____

_____

Date: _____

Body Weight: _____

Exercise   Weight   Sets   # of Reps

BBS_____

GB_____

CR_____

DP_____

DF_____

MDP_____

SUR_____

PU_____

SCR_____

SP_____

PO_____

SM_____

_____

_____

_____

_____

_____

_____

Date: _____

Body Weight: _____

<u>Exercise</u>   <u>Weight</u>   <u>Sets</u>   <u># of Reps</u>

BBS_____

GB_____

CR_____

DP_____

DF_____

MDP_____

SUR_____

PU_____

SCR_____

SP_____

PO_____

SM_____

_____

_____

_____

_____

_____

_____

Date: _____

Body Weight: _____

Exercise	Weight	Sets	# of Reps
BBS_____			
GB_____			
CR_____			
DP_____			
DF_____			
MDP_____			
SUR_____			
PU_____			
SCR_____			
SP_____			
PO_____			
SM_____			

_____

_____

_____

_____

_____

_____

"Golf Fitness" by Team Golfwell

Date: _____

Body Weight: _____

Exercise	Weight	Sets	# of Reps
BBS			
GB			
CR			
DP			
DF			
MDP			
SUR			
PU			
SCR			
SP			
PO			
SM			

"Golf Fitness" by Team Golfwell

Date: _____

Body Weight: _____

Exercise	Weight	Sets	# of Reps
BBS			
GB			
CR			
DP			
DF			
MDP			
SUR			
PU			
SCR			
SP			
PO			
SM			

_____

_____

_____

_____

_____

_____

Date: _____

Body Weight: _____

Exercise	Weight	Sets	# of Reps

BBS_____

GB_____

CR_____

DP_____

DF_____

MDP_____

SUR_____

PU_____

SCR_____

SP_____

PO_____

SM_____

_____

_____

_____

_____

_____

_____

"Golf Fitness" by Team Golfwell

Date: _____

Body Weight: _____

Exercise   Weight   Sets   # of Reps

BBS_____

GB_____

CR_____

DP_____

DF_____

MDP_____

SUR_____

PU_____

SCR_____

SP_____

PO_____

SM_____

_____

_____

_____

_____

_____

_____

Date: _____

Body Weight: _____

Exercise   Weight   Sets   # of Reps

BBS_____

GB_____

CR_____

DP_____

DF_____

MDP_____

SUR_____

PU_____

SCR_____

SP_____

PO_____

SM_____

_____

_____

_____

_____

_____

_____

Date: _____

Body Weight: _____

Exercise	Weight	Sets	# of Reps
BBS_____
GB_____
CR_____
DP_____
DF_____
MDP_____
SUR_____
PU_____
SCR_____
SP_____
PO_____
SM_____

_____

_____

_____

_____

_____

_____

Date: _____

Body Weight: _____

Exercise   Weight   Sets   # of Reps

BBS_____

GB_____

CR_____

DP_____

DF_____

MDP_____

SUR_____

PU_____

SCR_____

SP_____

PO_____

SM_____

_____

_____

_____

_____

_____

_____

Date: _____

Body Weight: _____

Exercise   Weight   Sets   # of Reps

BBS_____

GB_____

CR_____

DP_____

DF_____

MDP_____

SUR_____

PU_____

SCR_____

SP_____

PO_____

SM_____

_____

_____

_____

_____

_____

_____

Date: _____

Body Weight: _____

Exercise	Weight	Sets	# of Reps
BBS			
GB			
CR			
DP			
DF			
MDP			
SUR			
PU			
SCR			
SP			
PO			
SM			

Date: _____

Body Weight: _____

Exercise	Weight	Sets	# of Reps
BBS_____
GB_____
CR_____
DP_____
DF_____
MDP_____
SUR_____
PU_____
SCR_____
SP_____
PO_____
SM_____

_____

_____

_____

_____

_____

_____

Date: _____

Body Weight: _____

Exercise   Weight   Sets # of Reps

BBS_____

GB_____

CR_____

DP_____

DF_____

MDP_____

SUR_____

PU_____

SCR_____

SP_____

PO_____

SM_____

_____

_____

_____

_____

_____

_____

Date: _____

Body Weight: _____

Exercise	Weight	Sets	# of Reps

BBS_____

GB_____

CR_____

DP_____

DF_____

MDP_____

SUR_____

PU_____

SCR_____

SP_____

PO_____

SM_____

_____

_____

_____

_____

_____

_____

Team Golfwell's Other Books

Absolutely Hilarious Adult Golf Joke Book

Team at Golfwell's Other Books

FASCINATING GOLF STORIES
AND MORE HILARIOUS
ADULT GOLF JOKES
Another Golfwell Treasury
of the Absolute Best in Golf
Stories and Golf Jokes

Team at Golfwell.Net

Fascinating Golf Stories and More Hilarious Adult Golf Jokes

(Second in the Golfwell Adult Joke Book Series)

Team at Golfwell's Other Books

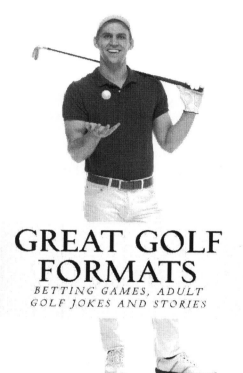

Great Golf Formats: Betting Games, Adult Golf Jokes and Stories

(Third in the Golfwell Adult Joke Book Series)

Team at Golfwell's Other Books

Golf Shots: How To Easily Learn a Wide Variety of Shots

Team at Golfwell's Other Books

Golf Driving Techniques from Golfing Greats and Golf Stories

Team at Golfwell's Other Books

Golf Putting Techniques from Golfing Greats: Proven Putting Techniques from Tiger, Rory, Jason Day, Jordan Spieth, and Others

Team at Golfwell's Other Books

Why Do Little Fat Ladies Beat Me at Golf?

How to Correct Common Golf Mistakes

Team at Golfwell's Other Books

Walk the Winning Ways of Golf's Greatests

Team at Golfwell's Other Books

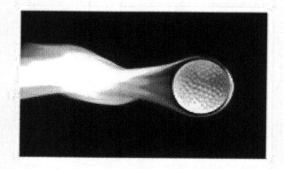

TEAM GOLFWELL

GOLF TIPS

AND ADULT GOLF JOKES

Golf Tips and Adult Golf Jokes

(Fourth in Golfwell Adult Joke Book Series)

A final message to you from The Team at Golfwell:

We hope this book made golf more enjoyable for you. Above all, have fun playing golf and enjoy all your adventures!

If you liked our book, please give it a review on Amazon.

Thank you for reading and best to you!

Info@TeamGolfwell.com

More about the Team at Golfwell

59616441R00126

Made in the USA
San Bernardino, CA
05 December 2017